Corporate culture : what it is and how to change it

Edgar H Schein, Sloan School of Management

Nabu Public Domain Reprints:

You are holding a reproduction of an original work published before 1923 that is in the public domain in the United States of America, and possibly other countries. You may freely copy and distribute this work as no entity (individual or corporate) has a copyright on the body of the work. This book may contain prior copyright references, and library stamps (as most of these works were scanned from library copies). These have been scanned and retained as part of the historical artifact.

This book may have occasional imperfections such as missing or blurred pages, poor pictures, errant marks, etc. that were either part of the original artifact, or were introduced by the scanning process. We believe this work is culturally important, and despite the imperfections, have elected to bring it back into print as part of our continuing commitment to the preservation of printed works worldwide. We appreciate your understanding of the imperfections in the preservation process, and hope you enjoy this valuable book.

HD28
.M414
no.1522-83

WORKING PAPER
ALFRED P. SLOAN SCHOOL OF MANAGEMENT

Corporate Culture:
What It Is And How To Change It

Edgar H. Schein
Sloan Fellows Professor of Management
Sloan School of Management
Massachusetts Institute of technology

ONR TR-26
November, 1983

MASSACHUSETTS
INSTITUTE OF TECHNOLOGY
50 MEMORIAL DRIVE
CAMBRIDGE, MASSACHUSETTS 02139

Corporate Culture:
What It Is And How To Change It

Edgar H. Schein
Sloan Fellows Professor of Management
Sloan School of Management
Massachusetts Institute of technology

ONR TR-26
November, 1983   *1522-83*

Invited address delivered to the 1983 Convocation of the Society of Sloan Fellows, MIT, October 14, 1983.

- Approved for public release: distribution unlimited.

- Reproduction in whole or in part is permitted for any purpose of the United States Government.

- This research is sponsored by:
    Chief of Naval Research,
    Psychological Sciences Division,
    Organizational Effectiveness Research,
    Office of Naval Research (Code 452),
    Arlington, VA 22217
  under Contract Number N00014-80-C-0905; NR 170-911.

CORPORATE CULTURE: WHAT IT IS AND HOW TO CHANGE IT
EDGAR H. SCHEIN
SLOAN FELLOWS PROFESSOR OF MANAGEMENT
SLOAN SCHOOL OF MANAGEMENT, MIT

Invited address delivered to the 1983 Convocation of the Society of Sloan Fellows, MIT, Oct. 14, 1983.

A few years ago the concept of corporate or organizational culture was hardly mentioned by anyone but a few social scientists. Today it is one of the hottest topics around because, it is alleged, a better understanding of how to build the right kind of culture or a strong culture will solve some of our productivity problems. Several recent books, most notably the Peters and Waterman (1982) report on the McKinsey study of excellent American companies, emphasize that "strong cultures" are a necessary ingredient of excellence. So the hunt is on to find strong cultures, and, thereby, fix our problems.

The dilemma is that we dont know exactly what we are hunting for. And it is not at all clear that we would know what to do with the catch if we found it. All kinds of definitions of organizational culture can be found, and all kinds of models are advocated for creating, managing, changing or even circumventing culture, just in case culture turns out to be an unfriendly animal.

Even if we learn how to decipher organizational culture, it is not at all clear whether full knowledge of one's own culture is always helpful. Sometimes self-insight is a source of anxiety and discouragement, and sometimes self-insight destroys the mystique of what we have. On the other hand, lack of insight into one's own culture leaves one vulnerable to forces of evolution and change which one does not understand and may have difficulty controlling.

One can see this clearly in the introduction of new technologies and processes such as the information, control, and decision support systems which the computer has made possible. Such systems have the effect of forcing managers and employees to confront aspects of their culture which they had never thought about before. For example, the introduction of electronic mail makes managers confront the question of how they prefer to relate to each other and what assumptions they hold about decision making. In one organization I know of, managers came to realize that they depended on face-to-face contact and frequent meetings. Instead of changing their style, they chose to hold on to this way of working and, instead, subverted the electronic mail system.

In another organization, the introduction of personal computers on all executive desks made it possible for senior managers to be fully informed about all aspects of their organization, a power which they used to question lower levels about any deviations they noticed. This produced so much resentment, hiding of information, and even falsifying of information, that the system had to be modified to introduce time delays into the information flow. Senior management saw data one day later than lower levels to allow them to investigate and find out why things were off.

The whole system of trust, delegation, management by objectives, development of subordinates, and getting decisions made close to the point of action, can be unwittingly undermined by the attempt to introduce some new technologies and practices. If we do not have insight into such consequences, we may change our organizations in ways that are neither desirable nor effective in the long run.

Insight into cultural matters also clearly affects the creation and implementation of strategy. Not only does culture limit the strategic options which are conceivable to an organization, but clearly one cannot implement strategies if they run against powerful cultural assumptions. One sees this most clearly in the transition from an engineering based to a marketing based organization. Not only is it difficult for the ex-engineer to conceive of marketing in the way that the professional marketer perceives this function, but the implementation of a marketing strategy may be undermined by the kind of people who are in the sales force, the incentive systems operating, the issues that executives pay attention to, and so on.

Yet the economic situation of an organization may dictate a strategy which requires some culture change, so we need insight into how to manage and change culture. But we must not forget that culture as a concept was invented by anthropologists to describe those elements of a social system which were, in many senses, the LEAST changeable aspects of that system.

How then shall we proceed to make sense of this area and to develop some useful insights for the management of organizations? I would like to approach these issues today by reviewing a model of corporate culture which emphasizes how culture is learned. If we are to influence the dynamics of culture change, we must first have a clear model of culture origins.

A DYNAMIC MODEL OF ORGANIZATIONAL CULTURE

The simplest way to think about the culture of any group or social unit is to think of it as the sum total of the collective or shared learning of that unit, as it develops its capacity to survive in its external environment and to manage its own internal affairs. Culture is the solution to external and internal problems which have worked consistently for a group and are therefore taught to new members as the correct way to perceive, think about, and feel in relation to those problems.

The kinds of problems which any group faces are shown in Chart 1. Think of a company that has just been formed or a new organization based on a merger. This new social unit must develop, if it is to survive in its external environment: 1) a sense of its own mission or primary task, some reason for existing. From this is typically evolved 2) some concrete goals, 3) some means for accomplishing those goals, by which I mean the organizational structures and decision processes which are developed, 4) some means of monitoring progress, the information and control systems that are utilized, and 5) some means of repairing structures and processes if they are not accomplishing the goals.

In order to function at all, however, the group must have 1) a common language and conceptual categories, 2) some way of defining its boundaries and criteria for membership, which is typically embodied in the recruitment, selection, socialization, training, and development systems of the organization, 3) some way of allocating authority, power, status, property, and other resources, 4) some norms of how to handle interpersonal relationships and intimacy, what is often embodied in the terms style or climate of the organization; 5) criteria for the dispensing of rewards and punishments, and 6) some way of coping with unmanageable, unpredictable, and stressful events. This last area is usually dealt with by developing ideologies, religions, superstitions, magical thinking and the like.

Note that organizational culture embodies the solution to a wide range of problems. We must never make the mistake of assuming that when we have described one aspect of a given organization that is very salient, such as how people are managed, for example, that we have then described the whole culture. Such a total description should deal with each of the external and internal issues which have been identified.

I have also observed in those organizations that I know well, that they are to some degree integrated by even more basic assumptions which deal with broad human issues. It is probaly the human need for parsimony and consistency which drives us to these higher order concepts, dealing with fundamental matters of organization/environment relations, the nature of human nature, the nature of human activity and relationships, and, most important, the nature of reality and truth, embodying very fundamental conceptual categories about time, space, and the nature of things.

I call these ASSUMPTIONS rather than VALUES because they tend to be out of awareness, taken for granted, and basically viewed as automatically true and non-negotiable. Values are debatable and discussible; basic assumptions are not. We are up against a basic assumption when our observations or questions are treated as dumb, crazy, or too absurd to be dealt with, as when someone questions whether the world is round, whether it is necessary to make a profit, why one should not schedule more than one person at a time for an appointment, and so on.

Once a group has had enough of a history to develop a set of basic assumptions about itself, we can think of the culture as existing at three levels, as shown in Chart 2. At the most superficial level we have artifacts, the visible behavioral manifestations of underlying concepts. They are easy to see, but hard to decipher. If I see that every office has an open door, that people wander into each others' offices and argue a lot, what does that mean? The artifactual visible and hearable environment can provide clues but rarely does it provide answers.

The next level has more credibility. If I ask people questions about why they do what they do, I will elicit values and begin to understand the reasons behind some of the behavior. I may learn that doors are open because the President of the company ordered them to be open; he believes that everyone should always be accessible. I may learn that people chat with each other because communication is highly valued, and that they argue a lot because one is supposed to get agreement of decisions before acting. I may also learn that middle managers are quite frustrated because decision making is taking too long, but if they try to become more efficient and disciplined, 'something' in the environment which they cannot identify resists.

When I have a good deal of information of this sort I can begin to see why the organization works the way it does, and often improvements immediately suggest themselves at this level. But I have not yet really confronted the essence of the culture at all. The values I have encountered are themselves manifestations of the culture, but not what we could think of as the driving force or essence of the culture.

I believe that what really drives or creates the values and overt responses is the learned underlying assumptions. As a group or organization solves its collective problems it always operates with some world view, some cognitive map, some hypotheses about reality, and, if it has success in solving those problems, that world view comes to be seen as correct and valid. It changes from a hypothesis to an assumption, and, if it continues to work, it gradually drops out of awareness altogether.

Because of the human need for consistency and order, the basic assumptions gradually come to be coordinated into a pattern, assuming that the group has a long enough life for this process to happen. So what I really mean by culture, is the PATTERN of underlying ASSUMPTIONS which are implicit, taken for granted, and unconscious, unless they are deliberately surfaced by some process of inquiry.

For example, if I continue to probe in the above company, I will discover that the deep reason why it has open office landscapes, open doors and frequent meetings is the shared assumption that truth can only be determine by some process of testing ideas on each other. This assumption about truth is combined with the assumption that anyone can have ideas but no one is smart enough to assess his or her own ideas, not even the boss, hence mutual testing is the only way to determine truth, even if that takes time and energy.

By contrast, in another company that has many locked offices and few meetings, the basic paradigm involves the assumptions that a job is considered to be a manager's personal turf, not to be interfered with unless there is clear evidence of failure, and then only the boss has a right to intrude with suggestions and corrective measures. Whereas in the first organization there is information overload and frustration over slow decision making because too many people can get into the act, in the second organization there is frustration over the inability to get innovative information from one part of the organization to another. The suggestion that there should be a system of lateral communication simply never gets off the ground because it is assumed that one will threaten and insult the manager if one offers information when none has been asked for.

Assumptions can grow up about the nature of a successful product, what the market place and customers are like, which functions in the company really are the most important ones, what is the best form of organization, how people should be motivated and managed based on Theory X or Theory Y assumptions, whether or not individuals or groups are the ultimate unit of the organization, and so on for each area shown in Chart 1. It is the interlocking of these assumptions into a basic paradigm which is the deep and most important layer of organizational culture.

HOW IS CULTURE LEARNED?

There are basically two learning mechanisms which interact:

1) Anxiety and pain reduction: the social trauma model; and

2) Positive reward and reinforcement: the success model.

Picture, if you will, a new group created by a founder. Such a group will encounter from the beginning the basic anxiety which comes from uncertainty as to whether or not the group will survive and be productive, and whether the members will be able to work with each other. Cognitive and social uncertainty is traumatic, leading group members to seek ways of perceiving, thinking, and feeling which they can share and which make life more predictable. The founder may have his own preferred ways of solving these problems which get embedded in the group, but only as the group shares in the solutions and sees that they work can we think of cultural learning (Schein, 1983).

In addition to these initial traumas, every new group will face crises of survival in its early history. As members share the perception of the crisis and develop ways for dealing with it, they learn to overcome the immediate pain, and also learn ways of avoiding such pain in the future. When a situation arises that is similar to a prior crisis, it will arouse anxiety and cause the group to do what it did before in order to reduce the anxiety. It will avoid as much as possible reliving the actual pain if it can be avoided by ritualistic ways of thinking, feeling, and behaving.

For example, if a young company faces extinction because of a product failure, learns that it has underengineered the product, and survives by careful re-design of the product, it may well learn that to avoid such trauma in the future, it should engineer products more carefully in the first place, even though that is more costly. Whatever works in "saving" the organization, becomes learned as the way to avoid future trauma. Members of the organization begin to think of careful engineering as "the way we do things around here," and teach new incoming engineers that "that is the way we should design products," based on the now unconscious assumption that this is the way to win in the marketplace.

The problem with this learning mechanism is that once we have learned to do something to avoid a painful situation, we continue to avoid it, thus preventing ourselves from testing whether or not the danger still exists. The company that now carefully engineers everything cannot find out whether or not customers now would or would not accept a less well engineered and less costly product. Trauma based learning is hard to undo, because it prevents us from testing for changes in our environment. Cultural assumptions learned by this means can then be thought of as DEFENSE MECHANISMS which the group has invented to cope with anxiety and potential trauma.

The second major learning mechanism is positive reinforcement. We repeat what works, and give up what doesnt. If the young company starts with some founder beliefs that the way to succeed is to provide customers good service, or to treat their employees as their major resource, or to always have the low price product, or whatever, and action based on that belief succeeds in the market place, then the group learns to repeat whatever worked and gradually accepts it as a shared view of how the world really is, thereby creating a piece of its culture.

But this learning mechanism is different from traumatic avoidance learning in that it produces responses which continually test the environment. If the environment is consistent in producing success and then changes so that previously successful responses no longer work, the group will find out about it quickly, and the responses will be re-examined and changed. On the other hand, this learning mechanism can also produce behavior very resistant to change if the environment is inconsistent, producing success at one time and failure at another time. Unpredictable intermittent reinforcement leads to very stable learning just as trauma does.

Learning theorists also note, by the way, that avoidance learning is so stable because not only does the ritualized avoidance response avoid the pain, but the actual reduction of the anxiety, the anticipation of pain, is very rewarding. Thus some organizational ways of thinking about problems produce the immediate comfort of anxiety reduction, even though those ways of thinking may be disfunctional in terms of adaptation to a rapidly changing environment. And if those ways of thinking have become deeply held, taken-for-granted, basic assumptions about the nature of the world, it is no small task to contemplate how they might change.

Once we have adopted a learning model of culture, the question of whether every organization has a culture can be answered in terms of whether or not it has had an opportunity for such collective social learning to occur. For example, if there has been low turnover of people, especially in key positions of influence, and a history of intense experiences with each other, a collective, shared way of thinking can be developed very quickly, as was often observed in wartime in military units. Thus, one could postulated that the strength, clarity, and degree of integration of a corporate culture or sub-culture is directly proportional to the stability of the membership of the group, the length of time the group has been together, and the intensity of the collective learning which has taken place during that history.

Notice, by the way, that if one adopts such a view of how corporate culture is learned, one cannot simply CREATE a strong culture by executive action. Such a culture evolves through shared history not managerial decisions to have a strong culture. Of course, one can always adopt the approach of a South African chief executive I know who created strong managerial teams by sending them off on a dangerous safari together. Whether such a model can be escalated to total organizations is something we can all speculate about.

This approach also deals with the problem of what is a sub-culture. Any group within an organization has the potential of developing its own culture if it has stable membership and a history of joint problem solving. Thus we would expect to find within a given organizations a variety of functional, geographic, rank level, project team, and other cultures which, from the point of view of the total organization can be thought of validly as 'sub-cultures,' just as the total corporate culture, if there is one, can be thought of as a 'sub-culture' vis-a-vis the larger society in which that company operates.

SELF INSIGHT AND CULTURE CHANGE.

Given this model of organizational culture, what can we say about the pro's and con's of obtaining insight into this deep level, and how does this relate to organizational culture change? The answer depends on the circumstances in which the organization finds itself, as Chart 3 illustrates. I am hypothesizing that the culture issue is different at different stages of development of an organization (Davis, 1982). I am also hypothesizing that the kind of change which is possible depends upon the degree to which the organization is unfrozen and ready to change, either because of some externally induced crisis, or some internal forces toward change (Schein, 1980).

Chart 3 shows three major developmental periods that can be identified in private organizations, and for each period hypothesizes what the major culture issues are, how much self-insight is crucial, and what change mechanisms are likely to be operating.

BIRTH, GROWTH, FOUNDER DOMINATION AND SUCCESSION

I am lumping together here a whole host of sub-stages and processes and am ignoring, for the moment, that this stage can last anywhere from a few years to a few decades. At this stage the organizational culture serves the critical function of holding the organization together while it grows and matures. It is the glue that permits rapid growth and the influx of many newcomers. One might expect to see strong socialization processes which become almost control mechanisms, and one might observe strong defensiveness around the organizational culture, because members recognize how critical the culture is as a force toward integration.

In this stage one can see the culture as a distinctive competence, and as a source of identity and strength. Assumptions about distinctive competence can involve the organization's products, processes, structure, or even relationships. For example, I know of a young and rapidly growing company in the lawn service business which has chosen their employees not their customers or stockholders as their primary stakeholders. All their truck drivers, secretaries, and maintenance people fully understand the economics of the business on the theory that if the employees feel totally committed and professional, they will see to it that customers are found and are well treated. The continued success of the business hinges on the ability to maintain such identification with the core mission on the part of a rapidly growing work force.

Self-insight is critical in that it is important for members to recognize what their source of strength really is, but the process of achieving that insight is not easy because one only wants to look at the positive and desirable qualities of the culture at this stage. A company may have gotten where it is by ruthless competition in the market place and ruthless internal weeding out of incompetents, but it does not necessarily want to accept that self-image as being its distinctive competence and source of strength.

During the period when the founder or the founder's family is still dominant in the organization, one may expect little culture change but a great deal of effort to clarify, integrate, maintain, and evolve the culture, primarily because it is identified with the founder. Culture CHANGE becomes an issue only under two conditions:

1) the company runs into economic difficulties forcing key managers to re-evalute their culture; or

2) succession from the founder to professional managers forces assessment of what kind of successor to pick.

How then does culture change happen in this stage? I believe one can identify four mechanisms:

1) Natural evolution, survival of the fittest;

2) Self-guided evolution through organizational therapy;

3) Managed evolution through selection of hybrids;

4) Managed evolution through introduction of key outsiders.

MECHANISM 1. NATURAL EVOLUTION. If the organization is not under too much external stress and if the founder or founding family are around for a long time, the culture simply evolves in terms of what works best over the years. Such evolution involves two basic processes:

a) General evolution toward the next stage of development, i.e. diversification, complexity, higher levels of differentiation and integration, creative syntheses into new and higher level forms. The elements of the culture which operate as defenses are likely to be retained and strengthened over the years.

b) Specific evolution or the adaptation of specific parts of the organization to their particular environments. Thus a high technology company will develop highly refined R & D skills, while a consumer products company in foods or cosmetics will develop highly refined marketing skills. In each case such differences will reflect important underlying assumptions about the nature of the world, and the actual growth experience of the organization.

MECHANISM 2. SELF-GUIDED EVOLUTION THROUGH ORGANIZATIONAL THERAPY. If one thinks of culture as being in part a defense mechanism to avoid uncertainty and anxiety, then one should be able to help the organization to assess for itself the strengths and weaknesses of its culture, and modify it if that is necessary for survival and effective functioning. Therapy which operates through creating self-insight permits cognitive redefinition to occur, and thereby can produce dramatic changes. Outsiders are necessary for this process to unfreeze the organization, provide psychological safety, help to analyze the present defensive nature of the culture, reflect back to key people in the organization how the culture seems to be operating, and help the process of cognitive re-definition (Schein & Bennis, 1965; Schein,

1969).

When this process works, usually because the client is highly motivated to change, dramatic shifts in assumptions can take place. I know of one company that could not make a crucial transition because of a history of defining marketing in very limited merchandising terms, and, hence, seeing little value in the function. This assumption, i.e. that marketing cannot really help, led to hiring poor marketers and losing the good ones which the company had. Only when key executives had real personal insight into how they defined marketing, and cognitively redefined the function in their own mind, were they able to adopt the assumption that marketing could help.

Much of the field of planned change and organization development operates on the therapeutic and self-insight model. The assumption has to be made that the system is unfrozen, i.e. there is motivation to change, and that there is readiness for self-insight however much pain that might entail. Organizations sometimes have to get into real trouble, however, before they recognize their need for help, and then they often do not seek the right kind of help. Sadly, organizations are no different in this regard from individuals.

This would model of change is, of course, a direct parallel to an individual changing life course or personality as a result of an intensive therapeutic process which emphasizes insight as critical. Powerful belief change can occur with cognitive redefinition. For example, in the studies of prisoners of war under pressure from interrogators to confess to crimes which they felt they were innocent of, the crucial change came about when the prisoner suddenly had the insight that his or her definition of crime, guilt, and innocence were all different from those of the captor. Once cognitive redefinition had taken place, i.e. recognizing that from the point of view of the captor certain previously unrecognized things were defined as crimes, it was possible to change one's view of oneself (Schein, 1961).

MECHANISM 3. CHANGE THROUGH HYBRIDS. One process which I have seen in several companies is captured by the feeling 'we dont like what he is doing in the way of changing the place, but at least he is one of us.' If the organization's leaders recognize the need for some change, but dont quite know how to get there, they begin to systematically select for key jobs those members of the old culture who best represent the new assumptions that the leaders want to implement.

For example, in one rapidly growing company there is the problem of moving from the assumption that the way to function is to all think for ourselves and exercise local option, to the assumption that the way to function is to make some decisions at the top and implement them in an efficient and disciplined way. To get to this way of operating the CEO has increasingly selected for senior management positions those younger managers who have grown up in and believe in the more disciplined ways of doing things, i. e. managers with a manufacturing background.

Formal management succession when the founder or founding family finally relinquishes control provides an opportunity to change the direction of the culture if the successor is the right kind of hybrid, representing what is needed for the organization to survive, yet being seen as acceptable 'because he is one of us' and therefore also a conserver of the old culture. An interesting special case is to create a hybrid by having an outsider who is being "groomed" as the successor to the founder serve for a number of years on the Board of Directors and becoming thereby partially acculturated.

MECHANISM 4. CHANGE THROUGH KEY OUTSIDERS. It is not uncommon in the succession process of a young and growing company to turn to outsiders to fill key positions on the grounds that the organization needs to be more "professionally" managed, that is, needs to bring in modern management tools which the founder is often perceived to lack. Turning to outsiders is also the most likely course if the company is in economic difficulty due to perceived inefficiencies associated with the old culture.

Gibb Dyer, one of our graduate students, has looked at this change mechanism in several organizations and has found what appear to be the key conditions for this process to work. Assuming that the outsider is really seen as different, not merely a hybrid, it would appear that the following scenario is prototypical--the organization develops a sense of crisis because of declining performance or some kind of failure in the marketplace and concludes it needs a new managerial approach; an outsider is brought in with different assumptions, many of which immediately conflict with the culture of origin, causing skepticism, resistance, and possibly even sabotage of the new leader's program. If organizational performance improves, and if the new leader is given credit for the improvement, he or she will survive and the new assumptions brought in will begin to operate. "We dont like his approach, but we cant argue with the fact that he made us profitable once again, so maybe we have to try the new ways."

If improvement does not occur, or the new leader is not given credit for what improvement does occur, he or she will be forced out.

DIVERSIFICATION AND ORGANIZATIONAL MIDLIFE

Let us look next at the cultural issues of organizational mid-life. It seems to me we are now facing a very different situation. The organization is established and must maintain itself through a continued growth and renewal process. Whether or not to pursue such growth through further geographic expansion, development of new products, opening up of new markets, vertical integration to improve its cost and resource position, mergers and acquisitions, divisionalization, or spin-offs becomes a major strategic issue.

Where culture was a necessary glue in the growth period, it is likely that the most important elements of the culture have now become institutionalized or embedded in the structure and major processes of the organization, hence consciousness of the culture and the deliberate attempt to build, integrate or conserve the culture has become less important. The culture that the organization has acquired during its early years now comes to be taken for granted. The only elements that are likely to be conscious are the credos, dominant values, company slogans, written charters and other public pronouncements of what the company wants to and claims to stand for, its espoused values and theories (Argyris & Schon, 1978).

At this stage it is difficult to decipher the culture and make people aware of it because it is so embedded in routines. It may even be counterproductive to make people aware of it unless there is some crisis or problem to be solved. Managers view culture discussions as boring and irrelevant, especially if the company is large and well established.

I would hypothesize that at this stage there may be strong forces toward cultural diffusion, toward loss of integration because powerful sub-cultures develop in the system, and because it is difficult to maintain a highly integrated uniform culture in a larger more differentiated organization. Furthermore, it is not clear how important it is for all of the elements of the culture to be uniform and integrated. Several conglomerates I have worked with have spent a good deal of time wrestling with the question of whether to attempt to preserve, or in some cases, try to build a common culture? Are the costs associated with such an effort worth it? Is there even a danger that one will impose a culture on a sub-unit which might not fit its situation at all? On the other hand, if sub-units are all allowed to develop their own cultures, what is the competitive advantage of being a single organization?

Geographic expansions, mergers and acquisitions, introductions of new technologies, all require a careful self-assessment to determine whether the cultures to be integrated or merged are, in fact, compatible. The major conclusion to be drawn about this stage, then, is that the cultural issue is complex and diverse. One might almost argue that in this stage there are so many different kinds of possible conditions which might require some management of the cultural issues, that executives of mature healthy companies should be required to understand as much as possible about cultural dynamics. If they then find themselves in a growth, diversification, acquisition, or merger situation, they would then have the necessary skills to diagnose and manage the cultural issues.

If external or internal conditions change and create a motivation for improvement, then suddenly the culture issue becomes relevant and salient. If the environment creates a crisis because of new competition, new technologies, changing market conditions, or socio-political changes, the organization may not be able to solve problems effectively. It only knows its own slogans and myths. Key managers now need a deeper level of self-insight into the content of their culture and into the cultural process that is probably going on.

Four mechanisms of culture change seem to me to be relevant at this stage in addition to the four which have been mentioned above:

5) Planned change and organization development
6) Technological seduction
7) Change through scandal, explosion of myths
8) Logical incrementalism

MECHANISM 5. PLANNED CHANGE AND ORGANIZATION DEVELOPMENT. Much of the work of organization development practitioners deals with the knitting together of diverse and warring sub-cultures, helping the dominant coalition or the managerial client system to figure out how to integrate constructively the multiple agendas of different groups (Beckhard & Harris, 1977). Thus headquarters/field conflicts, conflicts between functional groups, or, in a matrix, between functional groups and project groups, destructive competition between divisions, and so on, all require cultural understanding and the creation of interventions which permit mutual insight and the development of commitment to superordinate company goals. Such commitment always seems to involve both self-insight into one's own assumptions and insight into the assumptions of other groups with whom one feels in conflict.

MECHANISM 6. TECHNOLOGICAL SEDUCTION. This is a very large category which includes the diffusion of technological innovation at one extreme and the deliberate, managed introduction of specific technologies for the sake of seducing organization members into new behavior which will, in turn, require new values, beliefs, and assumptions, at the other extreme. For example, in situations where senior management sees too much cultural diversity, it often introduces a seemingly "neutral" or "progressive" technology which has the effect of getting people to think in common terms.

For example, many companies have introduced programs of leadership training built around notions like the Blake Managerial Grid (Blake & Mouton, 1969) in order to provide many layers of management with a common vocabulary and common concepts that make it possible to develop a more integrated uniform set of practices across diverse groups in the organization. The current practice of introducing personal computers to several layers of management, and the mandatory attendance at training courses may be intended to serve a similar kind of unifying function.

We should, of course, recognize that one reason why so many people resist such new technologies is because they sense that their cultural assumptions are being challenged and threatened. Technological changes not only disrupt our behavioral patterns but force us to look at and possibly change our underlying assumptions.

MECHANISM 7. CHANGE THROUGH SCANDAL, EXPLOSION OF MYTHS. It is not clear whether one should call this a mechanism or simply note it as one kind of event which can produce powerful culture change. As a company matures it develops a positive ideology and a set of myths about how it operates, what Argyris & Schon have labelled 'espoused theories,' while, at the same time, it continues to operate by other assumptions which they label 'theories-in-use' and which more accurately reflect what actually goes on. For example, an organization may espouse that it takes individual needs into consideration in making geographical moves, yet may make it virtually impossible for people to refuse an assignment because of the assumption that if one refuses, one de facto takes oneself off the promotional track. An organization may espouse that it uses rational decision making techniques based on market research in introducing new products, yet may find it impossible to challenge the biases and pet projects of certain key managers.

It is where such incongruities exist between espoused and in use theories that this change mechanism applies most clearly. Nothing changes until the consequences of the theory in use create a public and visible scandal that cannot be hidden, avoided, or denied. A senior executive, who has been posted to a position he did not want, commits suicide, and his note makes it clear that he felt the company pushed him into it. A product fails in the market place or turns out to be unsafe and members of the organization leak the fact that their own market research had shown the problem all along. Such events suddenly expose an element of the culture in such a way that it is immediately reassessed as incongruent. Strong policies are then immediately put in place to change the assumption which was operating.

The way in which I have described this mechanism it is more evolutionary than managed, but I suppose one could imagine scenarios where managers actually engineer scandals in order to induce some of the changes they want.

MECHANISM 8. LOGICAL INCREMENTALISM. Logical incrementalism means that in every decision area under the discretion of a manager, the decision is consistently biased toward a new set of assumptions, but that individually each decision is a small change. The concept was introduced by Quinn (1978) to describe what he saw as the actual process by which strategy is implemented in organizations. Key leaders do not create massive changes even though they have a clear concept of where they eventually want to end up. Instead they look for opportunities to make small changes, constantly test how they worked out, and concentrate on the opportunistic utilization of fortuitous events to move the system in a desired direction. Different sub-systems compete for their solutions and top management resolves the issue by selective support as the external situation requires it.

Such a process changes the culture slowly over a long period of time, especially if one set of such incremental decisions is the replacement of people in key positions by people with different assumptions. Executive selection and staffing processes are, in this sense, one of the most powerful processes of cultural change.

In summary, organizational mid-life is the period when managers have the most choice of whether and how to manage cultural issues, and therefore need to be most aware of how to diagnose where the organization is and where it is going. If organizations face increasingly turbulent environments, one might well advocate not STRONG CULTURES, but FLEXIBLE CULTURES, where flexibility hinges on cultural diversity rather than uniformity.

ORGANIZATIONAL MATURITY AND/OR STAGNATION AND DECLINE

The next and last stage to be considered is perhaps the most important from the point of view of culture change, because some organizations find that pieces of their culture or their entire culture become disfunctional in a dynamic competitive environment.

If a company has had a track record of success with certain assumptions about itself and the environment, it is unlikely to want to challenge or re-examine those assumptions. Even if it brings them to consciousness it tends to want to hold on to them because they justify the past and are the source of organization members' self esteem. Such assumptions now operate as filters which make it difficult for key managers to understand alternative strategies for survival and renewal, no matter how clear the strategy consultant's data and argument tend to be. Even if they are understood they often cannot be implemented because down the line in the organization the new concepts are not comprehended or accepted.

Unless survival anxiety is at least as high as the anxiety which accompanies giving up present cultural solutions, no motivation to change will be aroused. To put the matter metaphorically, if I have learned to fear dark rooms because I have always been punished by being sent to a dark room, I will avoid them whenever possible. But if I am being chased by a man with a gun and the only alternative is a dark room, I will forget my other fear and hide in it to survive.

For example, a company which has built its success on basic research now faces a world in which it is not clear whether there is much left to be invented, where patents have run out, and where younger more flexible competitors are threatening. The company needs to become more innovative in marketing, but the culture is built around research and the creative marketers have a hard time getting the attention from senior management which they need. The research department itself needs to become more responsive to the market place but it still believes that it knows best. Even those senior managers who can see the dilemma are caught in the culture in that they cannot really challenge and overrule the powerful research people. On the interpersonal side the culture dictates that a job is a person's own fiefdom. To ask for help, or to accept it are both signs of weakness. To offer help or information is potentially insulting in that it implies that the recipient does not know his or her job. Everyone is for change, but no-one knows how to get there, and the anticipated anxiety of real self-examination effectively keeps that from happening.

In this kind of situation the choices are between more rapid transformation of parts of the culture to permit the organization to become adaptive once again, what can be thought of as a TURNAROUND, or to destroy the group and its culture through some process of TOTAL REORGANIZATION via a merger, acquisition, or bankruptcy proceedings.

MECHANISM 9. TURNAROUND. The first condition for change through some kind of turnaround is that the organizational culture must be unfrozen. Either because of external realities which threaten organizational survival or because of new insights and plans on the part of the Board of Directors or the dominant management coalition, the organization must come to recognize that SOME of its past ways of thinking, feeling, and doing things are indeed obsolete.

If the organization is unfrozen in this sense, change is possible if there is 1) a turnaround manager or team with 2) a clear sense of direction where the organization needs to go, 3) a model of how to change culture to get there, and 4) the power to implement the model. If any of these is lacking, the process will fail. We know from organizational change theory that the key both to unfreezing and managing change is to create enough psychological safety to permit members to bear the anxieties which come with re-examining and changing parts of their culture. The turnaround management system must have the necessary insight and skill to manage all of the above mechanisms without arousing defensive resistance. For example, if major replacement of people in key positions is involved, that process must be managed in such a way that it is seen as necessary and carried out according to some of the deeper cultural assumptions which need to be preserved.

Effective turnaround managers use ingenuity and draw on all of the mechanisms reviewed so far. For example, one turnaround manager used technological seduction in the following way. A staid old delivery company was losing its competitive edge because it lacked a real concern for marketing itself. Its trucks were gray and had a royal seal painted on them, indicating its 100 year history. The company was acquired and a turnaround manager was put in charge. He decided that he wanted the trucks painted white, causing great consternation, but no one could think of a decisive argument to reverse the decision. Once all the trucks were painted, people in the street began to notice them and asked what would be put on the sides, getting employees at all levels involved in thinking about the nature of their business and how they would, in fact, advertise themselves. This is technological seduction at its best, but, of course, it also dealt only with a fairly superficial part of the culture. Deeper assumptions cannot be changed so easily.

Turnarounds usually involve the wide involvement of all organization members so that insight into the old culture and its dysfunctional qualities become clearly visible to everyone. The process of developing some new assumptions then is a process of cognitive redefinition through teaching, coaching, changing the structure and processes where necessary, consistently paying attention to and rewarding evidence of learning the new ways, creating new slogans, stories, myths, and rituals, and in other ways coercing people into at least new behavior (Schein, 1983). All the other mechanisms described above may come into play, but it is the willingness to coerce that is the key to turnarounds.

MECHANISM 10. REORGANIZATION AND REBIRTH. Little is known or understood about this process, so little will be said about it here. Suffice it to say that if one destroys physically the group which is the carrier of a given culture, by definition that culture is destroyed and whatever new group begins to function begins to build its own new culture. This process is traumatic and therefore not typically used as a deliberate strategy, but it may be relevant if economic survival is at stake.

SUMMARY AND CONCLUSIONS

I would like to summarize my analysis by drawing attention to five mistakes that need to be avoided in thinking about organizational culture. I will put them in the form of DO NOTS:

1) Do not oversimplify culture; it goes beyond slogans, behavior patterns, and values, to basic assumptions.

2) Do not forget how culture is learned; if traumatic avoidance learning is involved, remember that people will resist change.

3) Do not limit your thinking about areas of culture content; it goes beyond human relations into fundamental concepts of reality, truth, social structure and organization design, how decisions are made, and so on.

4) Do not assume that culture change is simple; it involves at least the 10 mechanisms outlined above and probably many more.

5) Do not assume that more culture or stronger culture is better; it depends on the stage of evolution of the company and its current state of adaptiveness. Instead of seeking that elusive, possibly non-existent, and possibly dangerous thing--a strong culture--try to understand and seek the strength of the culture you already have in your organization.

Keep you insight level high and face culture as a potentially friendly animal that can be tamed and made to work for you if you really understand it.

REFERENCES

Argyris, C. & Schon, D. A. *Organizational Learning.* Reading, Ma.: Addison-Wesley, 1978.

Beckhard, R. & Harris, R. T. *Organizational transitions.* Reading, Ma.: Addison-Wesley, 1977.

Blake, R. R. & Mouton, J. S. *Building a dynamic corporation through grid organization development.* Reading, Ma.: Addison-Wesley, 1969.

Davis, S. M. Transforming organizations: the key to strategy is context. *Organizational dynamics.* Winter, 1982, pp. 64-80.

Peters, T. J. & Waterman, R. H. Jr. *In search of excellence.* N.Y.: Harper, 1982.

Quinn, J. B. Strategic change: 'logical incrementalism' *Sloan Management Review,* 1978, 20, 7-21.

Schein, E. H. *Coercive persuasion.* N.Y.: Norton, 1961.

Schein, E. H. *Organizational Psychology, 3d ed.* Englewood Cliffs, N.J.: Prentice-Hall, 1980.

Schein, E. H. The role of the founder in creating organizational culture. *Organizational dynamics,* Summer, 1983, 13-28.

Schein, E. H. & Bennis, W. G. *Personal and organizational change through group methods.* N.Y.: Wiley, 1965.

CHART 1

ORGANIZATIONAL CULTURE

E.H. Schein

DEFINITION: Organizational culture is the pattern of basic assumptions which a given group has invented, discovered, or developed in learning to cope with its problems of external adaptation and internal integration, which have worked well enough to be considered valid, and, therefore to be taught to new members as the correct way to perceive, think, and feel in relation to those problems.

EXTERNAL ADAPTATION ISSUES (PROBLEMS)

Cultural elements derive from consensus on:

1) CORE MISSION, MANIFEST AND LATENT FUNCTIONS, PRIMARY TASK
2) GOALS DERIVED FROM MISSION
3) MEANS TO BE USED TO ACHIEVE GOALS
4) CRITERIA FOR MEASURING RESULTS
5) REMEDIAL OR REPAIR STRATEGIES

INTERNAL INTEGRATION ISSUES (PROBLEMS)

Cultural elements derive from consensus on:

1) COMMON LANGUAGE AND CONCEPTUAL SYSTEM - TIME AND SPACE CONCEPTS
2) GROUP BOUNDARIES, CRITERIA FOR INCLUSION
3) STRATIFICATION. CRITERIA FOR ALLOCATION OF INFLUENCE, POWER, AND AUTHORITY
4) PEER RELATIONSHIPS: CRITERIA FOR INTIMACY, FRIENDSHIP, LOVE
5) ALLOCATION OF REWARDS & PUNISHMENTS
6) RELIGION AND IDEOLOGY: HOW TO MANAGE THE UNMANAGEABLE

BASIC UNDERLYING ASSUMPTIONS

The essence of the culture will be the PATTERN of underlying assumptions dealing with the following core areas:

1) MAN'S RELATIONSHIP TO NATURE: ORGANIZATION TO ENVIRONMENT
2) THE NATURE OF REALITY AND TRUTH
3) THE NATURE OF HUMAN NATURE
4) THE NATURE OF HUMAN ACTIVITY
5) THE NATURE OF HUMAN RELATIONSHIPS

Different basic assumptions evolve to deal with the external and internal issues. Their inter-relationships and patterning makes up the cultural paradigm for a given group.

© 1983

CHART 3

ORGANIZATION GROWTH STAGES AND CULTURE ISSUES

GROWTH STAGE	CULTURE ISSUE, CHANGE MECHANISMS
Birth, early growth, founder domination, succession to "professional management"	1) Culture is the "glue" which holds the organization together; 2) Culture is source of identity and a distinctive competence; 3) Drive to integrate and clarify culture 4) Heavy emphasis on careful selection and socialization; 5) Potential successors judged on whether they will preserve culture; 6) Self-insight into culture critical. CHANGE MECHANISMS: 1) Natural evolution 2) Self-guided evolution through org. therapy; 3) Evolution through hybrids 4) Evolution through key outsiders.
Diversification and Organizational Midlife 1) New products/markets 2) Geographic expansion 3) Acquisitions, mergers 4) Vertical integration	1) Cultural integration declines as new sub-cultures are spawned; 2) Crisis of identity, loss of key goals, values, and assumptions; 3) Opportunity to manage direction of cultural change; 4) Decision for cultural uniformity or diversity; 5) Cultural self-insight important. CHANGE MECHANISMS: 1) Planned change and OD; 2) Technological seduction; 3) Change through scandal, myth explosion; 4) Logical incrementalism.
Organizational maturity, stagnation, decline 1) Maturity of markets 2) Stabilization of internal relationships	1) Culture becomes a constraint on innovation; 2) Culture preserves the glories of the past, hence is valued as a source of self-esteem, becomes a defense. 3) Culture change necessary and inevitable; but not all elements of culture can or must change; 4) Self-insight important in order to preserve essential elements of culture, avoid destruction of core. CHANGE MECHANISMS: 1) Turnarounds;

CHART 2

THE LEVELS OF CULTURE AND THEIR INTERACTION

LEVELS OF CULTURE

ARTIFACTS, CREATIONS
- Technology
- Art
- Visible and Audible Behavior Patterns

— VISIBLE BUT OFTEN NOT DECIPHERABLE

VALUES

— GREATER LEVEL OF AWARENESS

BASIC ASSUMPTIONS
- Relationship to Environment
- Nature of Reality, Time, and Space
- Nature of Human Nature
- Nature of Human Activity
- Nature of Human Relationships

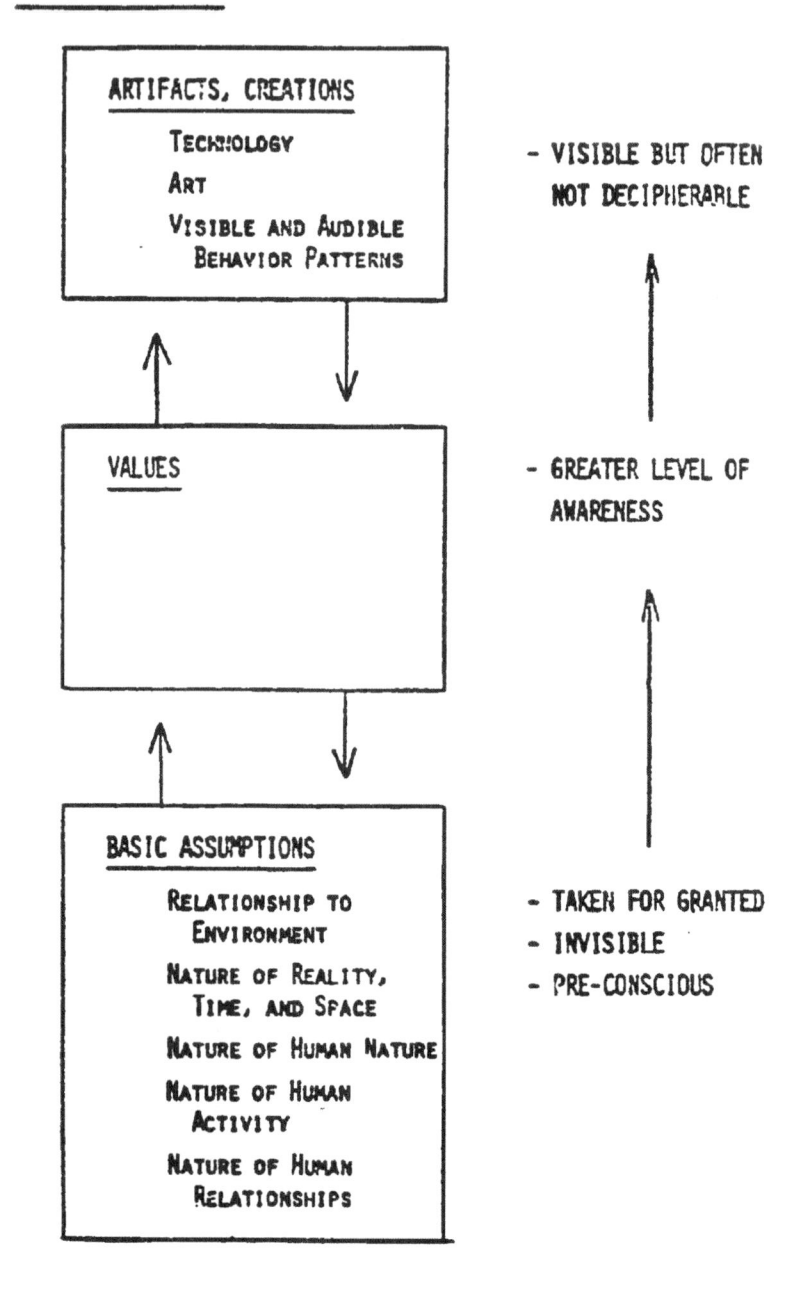

— TAKEN FOR GRANTED
— INVISIBLE
— PRE-CONSCIOUS

CPSIA information can be obtained at www.ICGtesting.com
Printed in the USA
BVOW10s1053241213

340020BV00010B/595/P

9 781175 748775